RAPID NON-FICTION

HOW TO WRITE & PUBLISH A HOW-TO BOOK FAST FOR PROFIT

JEWEL ALLEN

Rapid Non-Fiction
Copyright © 2020 Jewel Allen
Cover and interior design: Jewel Allen
First publication: May 2020

Special thanks to the following:
Robert J. Ryan, for your inspiring essay. Kathleen Brebes, Cotter Bass, Cathy Stucker, Kate Dixon and Rachel Risner for the valuable feedback. My sprinting friends for all the laughs while we are trying to be "productive." As always, my husband for your love and patience and not taking me too much to task for unrecorded receipts. Last but not the least, my Heavenly Father for giving me the opportunity to create stories.

Join my writing & publishing newsletter
for free writing tips and publishing updates at
www.JewelAllen.com/subscribe

Have you ever done or accomplished something and thought, "I should share with everyone how I did it"? Do you want to earn an income by publishing a non-fiction book—specifically a how-to book—quickly? Do you want to build your platform by writing a book on your niche for your current and future audience?

If one or all of those triggered a "yes," then this book is for you.

This is a no-frills book that spells out, step-by-step, how I wrote a short (20k-word) how-to book in three days that has not only hit Amazon bestselling lists but has remained "sticky" in its Amazon categories and has supplemented my fiction publishing income.

It's short and sweet and packed with useful advice you can act on right away.

As with any advice, should you take my experience

as gospel? I wish I could say yes, but really, you shouldn't. There are many ways to skin a cat, and this is just one of them.

Read, digest, and apply my takeaways. It's all here for you to use or discard. My hope is, it gives you information that I wish I had when I decided to embark on writing my own how-to book in January of 2019.

Who am I and why am I writing this book?

I have been a published fiction author since 2014, but before that, for 20 years, I was a journalist. As such, I learned how to write succinct, short articles that gave readers value. I learned to not be attached to a story that could quickly be tomorrow's fish-wrap or might end up being trimmed by my editor. The experience taught me invaluable skills, such as:

- Break it down in layman's terms.
- Don't talk down to your audience.
- Grab them from the start.
- Cut out the fluff.
- Get to the point.
- Don't show off.
- Build trust.
- Humor can be engaging but don't force it.

- Follow a sensible pattern but surprises
  are fun.

Eventually, I decided I wanted to try my hand at writing fiction, though non-fiction writing is my passion and first love.

In June of 2018, after publishing novels for four years, I attended a writer's retreat which changed my way of thinking as an author. I won't go into too much detail about that. It's all documented in my non-fiction how-to book, *Rapid Release: How to Write & Publish Fast for Profit.* But just to summarize, I decided to rapid release a clean billionaire romance series, one 50k-word book a month and chronicled how I turned a profit from the get-go.

Previously, I'd ghostwritten life stories as well as written travel memoirs and how-to blog posts, but I'd never attempted a full-fledged how-to book. My attitude was one of fearless naiveté, hopeful that a few people—namely some author friends—could benefit from reading about my experience.

To my surprise, "the little book that could" went on to earn an orange Amazon bestseller flag and even got me an Amazon author ranking in business & investing until I switched from 99 cents to full-price ($2.99). It's been a fun ride since, the benefits of which I will spell out in another chapter. There have also been a few eye-opening realities I had to learn the hard way. I'll dish those out, too.

As a former journalist, I live by the philosophy that a society with a robust exchange of ideas elevates everyone. So here's my contribution to a better writing and reading community. Enjoy!

SHOULD YOU WRITE A HOW-TO BOOK?

Here are some indicators you should write a how-to book:

1.You either personally experienced the topic, or

2.You have interviewed people who have experienced the topic, or

3. You have researched the topic and can put your unique spin on it

That's it. By all accounts, anyone should be able to write and publish a how-to book, right?

I am not a six-figure author (yet). But I *have* rapid released a clean billionaire series that, for the first time in my indie publishing career, I was able to clear a profit from the get-go.

I thought long and hard whether or not I should be the one to write a book about rapid release. Many other authors were and will be far more successful than me.

But I figured, if I don't, someone else will. Authors needed this book. I wanted to provide a solution sooner than later, so I went for it.

Whether or not your readership will take your offering kindly or negatively may depend on your level of expertise. Some people may be more impressed by author income or rank, awards, or number of books ... but it doesn't mean you shouldn't write a how-to book that a more successful author might tackle.

That said, I must warn you with a sad reality. You may get bad reviews. If you read enough of them, they might even paralyze you for a day or two until you are able to shake it off. But you may also get positive, encouraging reviews from readers who tell you thanks for inspiring them. I take the good and the bad and learn from them, and then move on.

Here's my personal philosophy when it comes to writing *anything*. If you write your advice in the spirit of being helpful and are careful to share accurate facts, then you should feel free to share it with the world.

~

How to be an "expert"

· · ·

Until your how-to book comes out, here are some ways you can establish your authority on your topic:

1.**Blog about it.** Some people say that blogging is dead. Not true. The *interactive* nature of blogging might have shifted to other venues like Facebook and Instagram, but blog content still makes an impact. For one, Google loves searchable material like text, and blog posts are easier to format than social media posts. I still read blog posts to this day to learn things, and I bet you do too.

For me, what has worked well to establish my non-fiction brand has been to do an author Q&A every week and post it on my blog. Once it goes live, I link it back to my social media to extend the reach of that content. It might not be much as a single post, but collectively, I believe they've made an impact on my searchability as an author. I have often had someone tell me, "I found your book through your blog post."

2. **Guest post for others.** Offer to write a post in your niche for another blog or for a popular Facebook page or group. Share with your circle so it is a win-win for you and your host.

. . .

3.**Network with others on social media.** People do notice those who are helpful and have something meaningful to say. Comment and ask questions when you can, related to your topic.

Nothing will establish you better as an expert than a book focused on a topic you're passionate about. The one person that you will need to convince the most you are an expert is ... yourself.

KEEP A DETAILED JOURNAL

If you are in the middle of the experience you want to write a how-to book about, you will want to keep a journal from here on. If you haven't started, that's fine. Just catch up.

I don't mean a paper copy kind of journal necessarily, though that is an option. You can type your journal entries in a Word document, or blog about it as I did. The advantage with a digital entry is you can copy and paste it into your book manuscript much more efficiently. The disadvantage is that sometimes what you have blogged about on the fly is clever enough for a blog, but as-is might not satisfy a how-to book reader.

Here are benefits of journaling on your non-fiction project.

- **Journaling gives you hard data and details.** When I started rapid releasing books in August of 2018, I blogged about my experience. I recorded my ranks, income, and the steps I was taking. I recorded the highs, the lows. Within five months of the start of that experiment, I had data. Data can give you credibility. Data is also handy when you are sitting there six months later trying to remember all things related to your experience.

Even little notes or lists on loose-paper on a clipboard may be valuable someday, when you finally narrow down your topic. The advantage of blogging is, depending on your topic, you have the potential of building an audience *before* you even write your book.

Here's another example. When my husband and I go on vacation, I stay up until two a.m. most nights writing down what we did that day. It's exhausting and sometimes I wonder why I am doing it when it's not an article that someone is paying for. But when it's time to put together our Shutterfly book, I have write-ups with the richest details just waiting to be incorporated into our photo book. What seemed like so much work during the vacation becomes a breeze later.

- **Journaling fine-tunes your writer's voice**, especially in a public forum like your Facebook page/group or a blog. I suppose some people might appreciate a how-to book written in a dry, nasally pretentious tone, but I would bet it's not a widespread preference. Journaling allows you to write unfiltered—and potentially funny—versions of your personal experience in a voice that sounds like you. You can then spot fakery in your writing and can scrap it before it spreads into a nasty mess. Blogging in public also forces you to not be boring. A good trait for an author to aspire to, wouldn't you agree?

- **Journaling gets you in a writing habit.** Writing is a muscle. To make it stronger, you need to exercise it. Writing a book is a marathon, not a sprint, and can be overwhelming even for more seasoned authors. The more you write, the easier words will flow when they matter.

- **Journaling gives you potential material for your first draft.** When I started drafting *Rapid Release* in January of 2019, I realized I already had the bare bones of a how-to book. I pulled in all my blog posts, broke them up into chapters, filled in a few more chapters, re-organized as needed, and completed the manuscript.

"Wait," you say. "What if I haven't been blogging about it?" Then sorry mate, you're doomed.

Kidding.

Okay, here's the thing. You are at a slight disadvantage compared to your nerdy, data-keeping, fellow non-fiction writers who probably also keep their grocery lists in monthly folders, but all is not lost. Retrieve your data, however much or little starting now. It's going to be tempting to not squirrel away things related to a topic that hasn't even fully formed in your mind.

At the very least, make a detailed outline and the steps you took to accomplish it.

Because you'll need it for your how-to book.

Once you start journaling, keep your entries in a safe place. Here are a few other ways you can collect your thoughts other than on a blog: paper notebooks, apps (Evernote, Day One, etc.), and voice memos. Refer to the entries often as you draft your book.

PICK A TOPIC THAT SELLS

I am assuming that you picked this book up to learn about writing a how-to book that sells. Even if you don't give a hoot about earning a lot of money for your efforts, you will still have a cost—your time and the opportunities you are giving up—so you will want some return on your investment in writing your book. Besides, wouldn't you want as many people as possible to read it?

Then pick a topic that sells.

It seems pretty obvious. But sometimes, because a topic sounds so good to *us*, we get dazzled and pursue it anyway.

Take the topic floating in your mind and look at it objectively.

Is it a topic someone else would either find useful or interesting? Will there be a market for it? Can you write it fast enough to get it out there while there is interest? For example, a year ago, about this time, many more people were trying their hand at rapid releasing, but there were few books—including mine—devoted to the topic. It was a good time to launch a book on the topic. As I am finishing the draft of this book, the year is 2020, and the world is in the midst of a COVID-19 pandemic. A host of other topics are going to be on people's minds, which might or might not be good news for you depending on your chosen topic. But if it seems timely now, make a goal to write the book that will be helpful for someone now while the interest is there.

One way you can narrow down your topic is Publisher Rocket (formerly KDP Rocket), a paid service which shows you what kinds of books are hitting bestseller lists. Personally, I don't subscribe to Publisher Rocket, but I know of several authors who do and swear by it. I can see why. It can probably cut down on the time to do market research. However, I'm cheap, and, if you are like me, an author already paying on everything from editing to covers to a book-earnings app to a newsletter service, and the list goes on, I'm always trying to do things free first before forking out more money for yet another author service.

Here's another example that drives home why it's so important to strike while the iron is hot. I had a book topic in mind as a follow-up to *Rapid Release*, which would have made sense late last year but now seems irrelevant, and now I wish I'd written the book when I was inspired to do so.

Ah, but live and learn. Don't be like Jewel.

I've written other non-fiction books before where I thought the topic would be interesting to readers (Who doesn't want to read essays about a family going on an African safari?) until I published it to the sound of crickets.

Even if a topic might be promising, you have to recognize how realistic it is to write about. When I was drafting the early portion of this book in July of 2019, there was a 20-something U.S. Congresswoman who undoubtedly would make for a great non-fiction project. But she is reputedly a private person who may not grant interviews, so I pretty much nixed that subject in favor of something else easier for me to write.

My own topic for my first how-to book, *Rapid Release*, came about after I polled the members of a Facebook author group I run. Initially, I was going to write a book on how to write a clean billionaire romance. But my group overwhelmingly voted for rapid release over it.

I was between books at that time, luckily, or I probably wouldn't have considered writing it. After a crazy

Christmas of two book releases and a trip to Mexico with the family, I decided to take January off.

Take the month off, yeah right.

By the end of January, I'd not only drafted, but uploaded my how-to book on rapid release. It's a blessed case of the immediacy of self-publishing working in my favor. I got my book out before anyone else had put out a how-to on the subject. Which is lucky. I very well might have chickened out had I seen the other authors' offerings. That's why it's important to go with a topic that you know you can finish by an immediate deadline, say within the next three months. So you can put it out before someone else does.

A Topic Brainstorming Exercise

1. List the topics you have expertise on.
2. Cross off the topics you have no interest in writing about. Or, the thought of spending the next few weeks writing about it makes you break out in hives.
3. You should have (hopefully) at least one topic left on your list. If not, start over and think harder.
4. Now you will come up with a totally

different list. Write down an area of expertise you wish you knew more about. Chances are, other people have been wondering about that, too. Maybe it's a problem you wished you had a solution for. Brainstorm a list of questions people might have about the topic, or fallacies that everybody gets wrong.

5. You should now have two lists. Do any of the topics overlap? If no, keep thinking. If yes, congratulations, you might have something promising.

6. Once you have the combined list with the overlaps, look on Amazon and google your topic. There's a common adage that if there's no book on the topic, there's probably not a market for it. That's not necessarily true. It's probably a niche that needs a book.

7. Let's say you're on Amazon and you're seeing a lot of books on the same topic. You have a choice to make. Either you will have to come up with a unique concept, or you might want to pick a different, less competitive topic. In your topic of interest, check the books' Amazon rank. If it hovers in the 20,000 range or less, it's got

potential. The lower the rank number, the better.

8. Do your market research. If you see there's not a book on repairing white calculators, and that topic excites you, you can simply ask, "But will anyone else get excited about it?" Ask your family, at the very least. Ask your neighbors. Ask people in the industry you want to write about. Pay attention to what Facebook forums are discussing.

9. Keep mum...for now. Although I am all about sharing information freely, I suggest you refrain from asking in huge public groups on the internet to prevent someone from mining your survey for a book idea for themselves. Don't worry, you'll reveal your book idea soon enough.

Once you've narrowed down your topic, you're ready for the next step.

PICK A GREAT TITLE

A great title can really make or break your book... unless you are a celebrity, in which case you could use "Me" with your photo on the cover and it would still sell millions of copies.

The rest of us aren't as lucky, so we have to be more creative. Unfortunately, some titles out there are either awkward, unintentionally cheesy, or unclear.

Avoid those.

(On the flipside, intentionally cheesy might pay dividends.)

I have seen some titles that, after a quick glance, convey what the book is all about. A short, succinct title that is easy to remember and rolls off the tongue prettily is a plus. Check out books on advertising on Amazon. Whoever brainstorms those books are masters at memorable, evocative titles. The best how-to titles include a benefit. Avoid titles that are overly clever or cute.

Personally, I like alliteration, where the start of each word or nearby words sounds the same or similar. When I was thinking of a title for *Rapid Release*, I googled the term. It comes up as a term related to massage therapy, but in publishing circles it is quite well-known. ***R**apid **R**elease* ... the title couldn't be more perfect.

Next, check on whether or not it's already a published book title. Is it already a claimed website URL? If your answer is no to both, then you may just have a winner.

But you're not done, just yet. You can entice more readers through a clever and clear subtitle. Amazon allows that option, and it can be a great search keyword for your book.

For example, with *Rapid Release*, I picked the subtitle *How to write and publish fast for profit*. That pretty much sums up what it's about.

Don't be wordy or convoluted. Some people think long is clever, when it just ends up...long. And cuts off in the Amazon preview so it's not worth adding a ton of words. Pick a title so someone knows clearly what the book is about.

Like one of my college English professors said, pick your words wisely. For *Rapid Release*, I didn't want to promise the moon. I knew, based on my data, that I had a profitable series, but "bestselling" would not have been as accurate of a term. So I went with profit.

Let the title roll off your tongue. If it sounds awkward, it probably is.

Finally, mock-up a cover with that title and study it to make sure it's not too long or too hard to get one or two lines. A title should also look good visually. In fact, I've often changed my title after I mocked it up because it didn't look so good on the cover.

If you are a DIY type of author, and you want to venture into making your own cover, read on to the next chapter. If you'd prefer to hire out the cover, go ahead and humor me and read on anyway. You might be surprised to learn a new thing or two.

DESIGN A GREAT COVER

You know your book best. Experiment with a concept initially and see where it takes you.

Let me use an example from my other life as a councilwoman for my city. Last year, I was running for re-election. I needed a campaign logo for a parade *fast*, so I designed my own. I kind of liked it, but I decided to get a designer to come up with another one for me. When it was all said and done, I ended up sticking with my design.

Somewhat sheepishly, I lamented to my husband that I could have saved her time and myself money had I just gone with my initial design.

"Trust yourself," he said.

That is my advice to you as well.

Trust yourself.

Can we both agree that you do not want a how-to

book cover that sucks? And that you want a cover that will sell books?

Here are some basic elements to consider. I will discuss them in further detail at the end of the list.

- A title with proper kerning (letters are spaced out evenly) and font.
- Colors that match or complement your author branding. (If you don't know what that is, don't stress about it. For now.)
- A catchy graphic that will draw your ideal reader. Or at least not repel them.
- White space.

1.Title with Proper Kerning

So first ... the title with proper kerning, or the spacing between characters. I usually will eyeball my title and make sure the letters are spaced out evenly. Also, I check to see if the title reads how I intended it. Sometimes, improper kerning could make your title read wrong or could be downright embarrassing.

One of the things I have learned to *never* take for granted is how the title looks in relation to the rest of the cover. Is it centered? Not too close to the edges?

Legible? Check in with a cover critique group and get their honest feedback.

2. Font

As for fonts, there are plenty of options that are free for commercial use nowadays. My go-to font website is Font Squirrel. You will want to experiment on which font gives you the best vibe for your book and is consistent with bestsellers in your genre.

Avoid cursive. Those usually don't come out legible. Look at the font objectively and make sure it's not a throwback from a past decade, unless you are writing about that decade.

How would you know what is modern and hip? Spend some time studying best-selling non-fiction books in your niche. Pick something similar but do not copycat.

Bottom line, don't overthink it to the point of paralysis. Pick a few fonts. Experiment. Note which one appeals to you as a non-fiction reader in that niche. Who is your target audience? Do you want the font to resonate to a mostly male audience? Female? Neutral? Both?

. . .

3. Colors that match or complement your author branding.

Branding is, in its basic sense, what a reader or viewer uses to form an opinion of you and your work. It conveys your professional persona, so choose well. Whatever you choose, it needs to be authentic and complement your books or there will be a disconnect.

For the first four years of my author career, I went through several iterations of branding. I went from an eighteenth century swashbuckling vibe to a simpler gold design to my current brand of my name in purple with a diamond solitaire. Just today, I re-branded yet again with a simple signature logo. I wouldn't be shocked if someday I change my branding to suit a new mood.

The reason I changed my branding the past couple of years is because my book covers had, as a collective whole, changed to include more contemporary romances. So I went with a softer, more feminine logo whose color and font I use consistently across my author sites and social media.

A whole book could be devoted on this topic, but branding is important so that all of your books and marketing materials look cohesive.

When you are choosing how to design your cover, match the color to your branding. I like to mock-up potential book covers into a series and look at them as a whole. I also compare each element so that they are symmetrical and visually pleasing. Repetition is a soothing quality. On the other hand, depending on your topic, you might prefer to be bold and unconventional. In that case, go for asymmetry or a not-centered look.

4. A catchy graphic that will draw your ideal reader. Or at least not repel them.

If you are a fiction author, you will know that it could take hours—days!—to find stock that could go on your cover to fit your story that has not been over-used. Non-fiction, on the other hand, has more options for vector art, which seems to work well for the genre. Such an easier process.

Here's how I picked mine: I looked at the best-selling writing books and noted their graphics and the placement on the cover. I then scoured stock photo sites to find ones that appealed to me personally.

You don't *have* to use a graphic, but I highly recommend it. Covers without graphics rely more on the font as a design element. Which is fine if you know what you are doing.

I designed the cover for *Rapid Release* and a few of my romance books but only because I came up with a workable concept. If I had mocked it up and it still looked dorky, you bet I would have gone to a pro for a design.

The one thing I would do differently on the vector stock art on my cover of *Rapid Release*, I would have picked either a vector model who isn't dressed in a jacket and skirt (I mean, what author does that unless you sneak writing at your office desk?) or I could have photoshopped pants on her.

Oh well, it'll be our little secret.

5.White space

White space is graphic design lingo that refers to breathing room on your cover so that the elements don't look cramped. It's not necessarily the color white, just space that does not have text or graphics on it. White space gives your eyes a place to rest so that certain things, like the title or graphic, could stand out.

Just like a workspace that is not cluttered looks visually appealing, so does a cover or art that observes this principle.

Bottom line...you *could* pay $30-100 (or more) for a cover. That's a totally legit way to go. In fact, a majority of authors probably really should leave cover design to the pros. The only thing I would caution you about this is, you don't want a cookie cutter approach to your cover. You know, that blocky placement of title that looks like every other how-to book. There is no rule that says you have to look like everyone else. In fact, if you don't, you just might stand out in a good way.

Before you plunk down money with a designer, see what you can come up with first, and get it critiqued by others. Go with a designer if needed. And then trust yourself.

6

CHOOSE THE PERFECT LENGTH

How long should your book be? Short answer: As long as it needs to be. I think anywhere from 20 to 50,000 words is a good length for a how-to book.

Personally, I like shorter how-to books so long as they give a reader value for the money.

Short or long, price your book accordingly. As I have been studying the non-fiction market I've noticed that readers will usually pay higher for reference books that they will want to read and re-read. Thus, the profit ratio is greater for a short work than a longer one. That said, you could earn more for a longer work if you choose to enroll your book in Kindle Unlimited, Amazon's subscription service that pays authors by the pages read.

But, and this is the big but, do not pad your book just to get those page reads. Make sure if you do add words, they are necessary. A common complaint I read on non-fiction reviews is that there's fluff in the text or most of it reads like an infomercial. I recently watched a how-to video that stopped about a third of the way in being helpful and turned into a sales pitch on a paying program. I quit watching right there. Avoid giving your readers a similar experience.

You will notice that I bring up book length before drafting your book. Even before you start, you need to know how many words you are aiming for so that you can plan your chapters and writing schedule accordingly.

What if you get to the end of your draft and your word count falls short of your goal? *Without padding,* go chapter to chapter and add any details or lists or instructions. Anecdotes, when relevant and if used engagingly, can be a good way to build up wordcount.

Or you could do Q&As with people in your field or ask experts to contribute an essay that supports your thesis. I did both for *Rapid Release,* adding another 8,000 words to my manuscript for a total of 20,000 words. To thank my fellow authors, I linked to their online URLs and listed them in the credits and blurb.

7

DRAFT YOUR HOW-TO BOOK

So...you've made up your mind to write your how-to book. Good!

How do you go about drafting your manuscript?

One word at a time.

A few years ago, I started a memoir ghostwriting business, which isn't *exactly* like writing how-to books, but the principle is similar. Here's the fool-proof method I use for drafting my clients' books.

- **Gather anything you have written so far on the topic.** Have you written blog posts in the past? Pull anything and everything in a sequence that makes sense and break it up into logical chapters.

- **Research and read widely on the topic.** As I embarked on writing about the rapid release method, there were literally no books out there on the topic. This made my job both easier (no risk of me plagiarizing someone else) and harder (no works to emulate or publishing gaps to fill). If there had been other books, I would have cursorily read them to get a feel for what is out there, but would have avoided reading them word for word to avoid copying, even subconsciously. As your goal is for your book to go out fairly quickly, do not get bogged down on research. Research enough to get your facts straight and get writing.

- **Fill out the rest of the book with an outline.** For example, for the rest of this book I made this list:

Fiction writing vs. Non-fiction writing
Sprinting

Get beta readers
Get a professional editor
Prepare a paperback
How to launch a book
Hitting a bestseller list
Pitfalls to avoid
Income from a How-to Book
Building on your book's success
Resources

I might or might not follow that outline to a T (for the record, I didn't), but outlining gave me a good starting point to make sure I don't miss any important points.

When you outline, you are better off making the list longer so that you for sure can hit your word count goal. You can always cut later when you're revising.

- **Using your outline, write conversationally in each chapter.** Why conversationally? Because the opposite is stilted and academic, which will most likely come across as a snooze fest. Let your personality show. Pretend you are talking to your favorite cousin who is visiting you. Have fun and don't be so formal. No one likes a pompous bag of hot air. Basically, you want to be likeable, so think of the traits that you like in a good conversationalist: casual, relaxed, clear, engaging. Don't worry about being proper, but don't be insulting. If you are prone to swearing, weigh carefully whether or not to do so in your book. I don't know how many times I have been sucked into a non-fiction book only to put it down because of profanity. It would be a shame to miss out on a slice of the market over something that may not be crucial to your message.

- **Make a guesstimate of how many words you would need to write and how many days it would take.** Create a regular, realistic schedule. I was able to knock out most of the 12,000 words of *Rapid Release* in two days by sprinting (read more of this in Chapter 11) because I needed to get on to a novel that was on pre-order. I had to plan my days accordingly, clearing my schedule.

- **Write on, even if most—if not everything—sounds hokey to you.** Whether the assessment is deserved or not, you just need to get your thoughts and words on the screen. You will be revising this later. All is not lost.

When in doubt, leave it in. You can always cut it out later. But don't be so in love with certain passages you aren't willing to cut it if that is what your manuscript needs.

- **Have a beginning, middle and end in the narrative.** Who hasn't had this drilled into them in a writing class? That's because the human brain likes order. Express your hypothesis or your plan in the beginning to manage reader expectations, support that in the middle of your manuscript, and end by circling back to a beginning thought or imagery. This will strengthen your narrative and pack a punch at the end. It also will help your reader arrive at the same conclusions as your book. That said, feel free to skip a section and go back to it as you draft your book. Agonizing over a section is not the best use of your time. Finish the easier ones, then go back to the problem ones.

- **Vary up the elements you use.** A succinct, relevant story nestled in blocks of how-to will keep your narrative engaging. Use a mix of short and long sentences. Use extremes in length sparingly. Using short sentences constantly will make the reading experience choppy. Long, unbroken sentences can potentially confuse and overwhelm the reader. But a mix of both may be interesting.

- **Save yourself and your editor time

by writing in the active voice. Some editors are real sticklers about this. Here are some examples:

Active: "The dog ate my homework."
Passive: "My homework was eaten by the dog."

Active: "The dog is a big jerk!"
Passive: "The dog was punished by my mom."

You can still use the passive voice; saying you never can is plain unrealistic. I mean, people talk in passive voice. Just don't over-do it. Your writing will exude more power if you use the active voice.

8

APPLY FICTION TECHNIQUES

Before I wrote novels, I was a journalist. It was a great training ground for storytelling. After several years, I learned to stitch together a coherent story on a dime to the wordcount needed or open with a great hook that my editor would usually leave untouched. (A hook is just that—a good piece of writing that hooks your reader.)

When I decided to write fiction, my newswriting also improved. My fiction-writing techniques started bleeding into my feature articles. I would craft a creative hook for my feature articles...and my editor loved it. I incorporated dialogue, suspense, and humor, among other elements, to make my feature articles more engaging. Crossing over from fiction to non-fiction or vice versa can help a writer grow.

Here's how to apply good fiction elements onto

non-fiction projects:

- **Open with a great hook.** Don't sweat it if your opening isn't as catchy as you'd like it to be, but do try for something more interesting than "Hi, my name is...." Here are some interesting openers. Ask a question. Make an outrageous observation. Launch with a punchy anecdote. Pick an interesting detail about a character and make it prominent from the get-go.

- **Use a consistent style or vibe.** If you are aiming for a funny tone, your manuscript should reflect that throughout. Be consistent. If you are breezy and casual, keep this style throughout. You can indicate this with your choice of words and tone.

- **Keep your paragraphs on the short (but not choppy) side.** It's hard to get excited about long blocks of text on a page. Your readers will be better able to digest the information in smaller doses. Earlier, I'd mentioned about white space being an important element of a cover. Same with text. Give the reader a place to take a break and to rest their eyes.

- **Incorporate dialogue.** Dialogue livens up your narrative and breaks up blocks of text. Some people have a great way of saying something, so take advantage of that to add color to your story. You can paraphrase some dialogue, but non-fiction is just that, your version of the truth. So try to stick to what really happened, instead of making things up. It's not just ethical to be honest, but it's also going to prevent potentially embarrassing situations when you are quoted contradicting something you said in your book.

- **Use all five senses.** I tell my kids this

all the time, when they are traveling and writing home. Using the senses makes the scene come alive, especially for someone that has never experienced it before.

What did the air smell like? What sounds did you hear? How did the cloth feel under your fingertips? What did the lamb stew taste like? What were the colors and sights?

Pick out details and isolate them. For one of my feature articles, I interviewed a singer in his Reno hotel. As I entered the room, he stood backlit against curtains that kept the room dark from the afternoon sun. He reached up and pushed the fabric to the sides, letting the light in. I opened and ended my article with that powerful scene detail, and my editor loved it.

Fiction vs. Non-fiction Writing

For all the advantages of being cross-trained in fiction and non-fiction, I must say, non-fiction writing is not *just like* writing fiction. Some things that work in fiction could make a reader expel a breath of impatience and not slog through your book. Here are some differences worth noting between fiction and non-fiction, and what you should do for a how-to:

- **Don't beat around the bush.** Unless you are a short fiction writer, you may be able to write an epic-length book with elaborate settings and characterizations and plotlines. With non-fiction writing, you can put in some anecdotes, but essentially, you need to get straight to the point. Your readers are busy and they need your information *now*.

- **You cannot simply make things up.** Well, I guess you can admit to making things up, but for the most part, stick with the facts. I cannot stress enough that one slip-up—however unintentional—could put your credibility in question and jeopardize a potentially successful publishing career. It's easy to slip-up due to laziness. *If* this ever happens to you, because, let's face it, no one's perfect, admit it with transparency and move on. And try to avoid it next time by going over your manuscript carefully.

- **Be honest**. Fiction writers are masters at the sleight of hand. They pull a plot twist at the end of the story that has the reader gasping over the cleverness. Clever as that may be, non-fiction readers appreciate being told upfront what the book will do for them, and expect the book to deliver accordingly. You can play around a little as to the delivery of this, but you can have spoilers at the start of your book, and it would be okay.

- **Write standalone chapters.** Fiction readers usually read in a linear fashion whereas non-fiction readers skip around to what they need to know about *now*. As you craft your chapters, guide your readers by suggesting chapters to read next depending on their interest. As an example, I mentioned that earlier in the chapter leading to DIY covers. This technique makes me think of those "pick your adventure" type of stories. If a reader skips to a section, no need to be offended. Hopefully, they will find it and still have a pleasant impression of your book overall because you helped solve their problem.

- **Keep your instructions simple**. Fiction writing can involve lush and elaborate word formations. And that's good. Through fiction, you can weave a magic spell and lure your reader into an escapist world. That is a different skill, however, than say, showing someone how to clean a floor using a mop. If you took the time to over-indulge and explain how one of your ancestors was accused of being a witch at the Salem Witch Trials, then you might have more respect for a broom over a mop...get my drift? What might be entertaining in fiction can be plain fatiguing in a how-to book.

9

READY, GET SET, SPRINT!

Here's some good news. Drafting a non-fiction project could be tons easier than a fiction project. I've done both, and to me writing non-fiction can be a breeze, especially if I am passionate about my topic. Whereas with fiction, I have gone into a manuscript with some bluster only to be driven to my knees near the end of the book because I feel like a woman suddenly gone blind on a freeway.

Non-fiction is easier, that is, once you get over the hurdle of worrying whether or not you have the world's permission to be an expert on the subject.

Yup, no pressure.

The other good news is, if you write your non-fiction manuscript fast, you won't have time to obsess over that pressure.

The hardest thing may be gaining that discipline to

write and eventually finish your non-fiction book. This is where sprints come in.

But first, let's talk about what sprints are trying to overcome.

When I was in high school, I was lousy at math. Physics was not my strong suit, but I do remember one principle from that long semester that passed me by in a haze: inertia. It's a lot harder to get a still object to budge than one that is already moving.

Inertia in writing means there will be some mornings when you don't want to write your draft and you will suddenly think of a million other things that could occupy your time, like hobbies you decide to pick up, so when the FedEx guy arrives in the early afternoon, you are still in your jammies without making any progress towards your non-fiction bestseller.

Just start.

That's it.

Make sure your family is fed and the dog has gone potty outside and the crockpot started, and just start. Write for fifteen minutes, an hour, or longer. Best if you keep at it for a short period of days, especially for a shorter book. Here are some advantages of sprinting a non-fiction book:

1. If you've outlined, you already know the
   plot of your book. Write the first chapter,

the next, and the next, and before long you will have your book written.

2. Writing it fast will encourage you to write in that conversational tone that will be more relatable to your readers.

3. You will finish your book and can earn money faster. Fist pump!

4. You can edit it faster, making you want to tear your hair out too...oh, wait. Seriously though, the faster you can edit it, the sooner you can get to other projects. Wouldn't that be fun?

I've sprinted both fiction and non-fiction projects, and essentially the sprinting principles are the same. Here are some techniques that have worked for me. They are also covered in my book *Rapid Release*, but I may have learned a new thing or two since:

1. **Find a supportive group with a good level of seriousness.** There are many awesome groups on Facebook. In one I am a member of, sprints on Zoom have become a thing, which can be fun if you like being social. As for me, I sprint best when everyone shows up to get some serious wordcounts down. When I lead a

sprint on Facebook, I say what time I will start a 20 minute sprint, say, at :00 (since we are all on different time zones, this keeps the time somewhat easier to track), set my phone clock, say "time!" at the end of the sprint and we all share our wordcount for that sprint. I'm kind of competitive, so a fast sprinter often goads encourages me to go faster.

2. **Experiment with sprint lengths**. I write for 20 minutes and then take a 10-minute break, writing at :00 and :30. I like the rounded numbers of :00 and :30. If I start on some other time, say, at :15, I spend half the time mentally trying to figure out when my 20 minutes is up. Some people like to sprint for 15 or 30. To me, 15 feels like I have to jump in and out of my train of thought to be productive, and 30 feels soooo long, but that's me. You may have to find your sweet spot by experimenting.

3. **Enjoy the breaks.** During my breaks, I chat with other sprinters, check my Facebook timeline, dash around doing chores, feed the animals, grab a quick bite, call my mother. Not only does this help me get things done in the house, it also gives

my brain the rest it needs so that I can be fresh for the next round of sprints.

4. **Keep your nails short.** Until the COVID-19 quarantine that shut down nail salons, I had been sporting manicured nails. I have dry skin, so a good manicure kept me from chewing my nails. It's March 2020 and I finally had to cut my over-long nails. Yowzah. I've gotten zippier on my keyboard ever since. I think next time I will get a manicure still, but keep my nails short.

5. **Listen to instrumental music.** I find it hard to concentrate when there are words in my background music. If it's too silent, I hear the cogs in my brain whirr too much and that gets me paralyzed too.

6. **Write in one long sitting if possible.** I will write either all morning, all afternoon, or all day, in a single stretch. I wrote *Rapid Release* in three days because I blocked everything else out and focused on getting my manuscript written.

7. **Get moving.** If you are not used to sitting and writing for a long time, this will be hard on your body. I used to rely on taking breaks between sprints but seldom

did so. What I did was to attach a little desktop on a cheap treadmill walk on it in slow mode for batches of time during the day. That way, I am getting my exercise while still keeping the thread of thought going in my head.

8. **Avoid over-snacking.** I admit to indulging in trail mix, cashew nuts and chocolate. But only after I have sprinted for a bit. Eating while sprinting can be distracting and slow your pace down. Just think of how many more words you could crank out during the sprint if you don't have to take the time to unwrap another candy bar.

9. **Record your progress.** A factual record of wordcount will keep you accountable and will indicate your progress or lack thereof. For me, 500 words or so per sprint is a good flow. Some people can sprint as much as 900! I have gotten up as high as over 1,000, usually when I am motivated by a deadline to get my book to the editor. As the words rack up, so will your confidence that this project will eventually come to an end.

How I measure my progress: I record the date, my starting and ending wordcount, calculate the difference, and write down the numbers in my planner. I used to write it down on loose-leaf paper, but that was too disorganized for me. I have also recorded wordcounts in a note app on my phone.

1. **Celebrate your achievements.** Share your wordcount with other authors on social media who will understand why that type of success matters. Or even your spouse who sweetly encourages even when he doesn't understand the whole of it. Post pictures on your author page. It builds excitement among your potential readers and builds content.

2. **Don't compare yourself with others.** Someone is bound to be faster or slower than you. Don't worry about them. So what if they're amazingly speedy? Good for them. Just focus on getting more words into your manuscript with every sprint.

3. **Do not edit as you go along.** Make notes along the margins or highlight portions where you will want to go back later. Avoid researching things too, because that will just bog you down. Again, make a

note and google later. Keep drafting and save revising for later.

4. **Stand once in a while.** This will keep the blood flowing to your brain and keep your body from feeling sluggish, which will help you sustain your marathon efforts. Take a brisk walk in fresh air if possible.

5. **If you are sorely tempted to give up on your project, don't!** Keep sprinting. It will sound lame in parts, you will feel inadequate, I get all that. Withhold judgment on the project until you have finished it and read it through in one sitting. You might just discover it's not as lame as you think.

6. **"Talk" your book.** You may find it easier to pretend you are telling your friend how to do whatever your book is about and "speak" to them instead of keying. Most computers (and even phones) come with dictation software or you can buy something like Dragon Naturally Speaking.

10

RECRUIT BETA READERS

A beta reader is a person who, usually for free, reads and gives feedback on your manuscript after you've done at least one pass-through revision. A beta reader can save your hide as an author of any book, but especially if you are writing non-fiction. They will deliver the good or bad news to you if your book A) makes sense and B) is actually helpful in solving a problem they are facing. So you would want to get a variety of beta readers that could help you determine both.

You need beta readers who are experts on your topic, people who are not experts on your topic, and everyone in between. Ideally, get one of each. Or, get beta readers with skills that complement each other's. For example, you might have a beta reader who focuses on the grammar and language, while another one focuses on content. Both are great.

Some things that could help the process go smoothly:

1. **Tit for tat…or not.** It is customary to trade beta reads with other authors, but if for some reason you aren't able to return the favor right now, just be upfront about it. You can also promise a beta read at a later date. The operative phrase is, you are *not obligated* to trade. If you would simply feel too stressed out to fulfill a trade, then look for paid beta readers. I have found groups on Facebook where betas offer a super-quick turnaround for a nominal amount.

2. **Ask for specific feedback from volunteer beta readers, while lowering your expectations.** Don't expect more than general advice, because they are doing you a free service. Some betas can be more generous than that, and if they are, consider yourself lucky. If you are new on the writing journey, a beta can help you polish your manuscript so that it can be ready for a professional editor (more on this in the next chapter).

3. **Ask your beta readers to be as**

honest as they can with you. Better to have them say something constructive at this stage then have it be mentioned in a review later. One of my beta readers for *Rapid Release* matter-of-factly said that my intro was long and frankly not very interesting. I swallowed my pride, thanked her, and realized she was right. I shortened the intro considerably and I was so glad I did.

4. That said, **take everyone's feedback with a grain of salt.** If more than one beta reader shares the same suggestion, then you are smart to take heed. Ultimately, however, you will need to decide for yourself if a certain change is necessary.

5. **It's normal to feel terrible**. You will probably want to cry and eat tons of chocolate the day you get back your beta reader's feedback. If so, cry and eat, and then take a deep breath. You aren't as terrible a writer as you think you are. If the advice is given in the spirit of helpfulness, take this as an opportunity to learn from others.

6. **Ask for one or two betas at a time.**

And then maybe add a second set. Too many cooks spoil the broth. The more feedback you have, the more confused you might get, especially if the advice conflicts with each other. Take the advice of few and trust your instincts.

7. **Thank your betas by acknowledging them in your book and giving them a free e-copy of the final version of your book.** Some authors I know give out paperbacks, which is a good gesture especially since it doesn't cost an arm and a leg.

8. **Before you ask a person for another beta read, be nice and beta read an equivalent length of work for them first.** Kindness goes a long way. Again, be realistic with your time.

11

HIRE A PROFESSIONAL EDITOR

If this is your first rodeo, you'll definitely want to hire a professional editor. Revising a document with the help of an editor will teach you what to watch for when writing a book, plus help start your career off on the right foot.

I have worked with a variety of editors and those I hire over and over do the following:

- They are tough but kind. They will not let you get away with things, but they will not belittle your efforts.

- They tell you the good and the bad.

Overall, they give you hope that you can make the edits you need.

- They don't spare you the grim news but give you feedback now to spare you from bad, bad reviews later (note there may still be bad reviews, but hopefully not as bad).

- They give you specific suggestions as to how to fix problems while still allowing you to retain your voice.

I've only been burned once by an editor who gave me bargain basement prices on an edit. Turns out you get what you paid for. They didn't give any constructive suggestions, everything was upbeat, and they cleaned up grammar and spelling. I suspect they simply put my document through a spellcheck and Grammarly and called it good. (Really, I'm not *that* good of a writer.)

How do you know which editor to hire? Ask your experienced fellow authors for recommendations. Put the editors on a scale from very cheap to very expensive and try to find someone somewhere in between.

In the spirit of transparency, I did not hire an editor for *Rapid Release.*

"What, Jewel, but you said—"

I know. I did. And I still stand by the premise that a good editor is gold.

However, I fount out that affordable non-fiction editors who give quick turnarounds are hard to find, and I aimed to rapid release.

If you go the editor route (which I recommend especially for those with minimal to no publishing experience) build in a bit of time to the process. At the very least, consider hiring a proofreader to catch those pesky typos before you release your book to the world.

But first, let's next talk about the dreaded R-word: Revising.

12

REVISE AND THEN MOVE ON

Sometimes, one can have too much of a good thing.

That also goes for revising.

Revising is a necessary step in the process of producing a book you can be proud of. But it can also paralyze you to the point that you keep delaying its release into the world. Like I pointed out earlier, rapid releasing non-fiction is beneficial if your topic can solve someone's problem *now*.

I used to hate revision with a passion. Used to dread it so much I would get physically ill. Eventually however, I discovered things that helped make the revision process more pleasant for me and for my editor.

Here are some hacks *before* your manuscript goes to your editor:

- **Before starting your book, construct an outline of topics.** Stick to it fairly closely so that the document will at least make sense and you will avoid repetition. For this book, I pulled the outline into the document and used each topic as my chapter heading as I went along.

- **If your narrative involves a timeline, double-check the dates.** A good editor should catch any inconsistencies, but you can make this easier to catch if you do some advance legwork yourself. As I write my manuscript, if a date is involved, I write, "Day 1, <short phrase describing events>" in the margin of my Word document. That way, I can see and confirm the timeline, and my editor doesn't have to do all that work.

- **Rename your document and read

through it in one sitting if possible. When I am in serious editing mode, I make notes in the margins if I have questions or need to check on something and then keep reading. I rewrite clunky sentences, catch typos, and keep an eye out for formatting issues. If I have to rewrite passages, I save those for later. My goal with the first pass-through is to get a feel for the book as a whole so that I have a general idea of what needs to change.

- **Read your document aloud.** I haven't done that in a while, but other authors swear by it. This step can definitely catch cringe-worthy, awkward sentences.

- **After that first pass-through, make final changes and then run the document through spell- and grammar-check.**

- **Confirm that your chapter numbers are correct**. If you are using chapter titles, keep them consistent. For example, for this how-to book, I decided to start the how-to chapter titles with verbs. A simple tweak that will make the book seem more organized.

- Congratulations! Now go **send it out to your editor.**

After your editor gives you your manuscript and you've had a good cry and some chocolate:

- **Take a deep breath.** It's not as bad as you think it is.

- **Block out uninterrupted time where you can sit and read your editor's comments.** Think about the suggestions for a few hours and let the solutions percolate in your brain. Sleep on it if you have to. Some emotional distancing will give you the power to make the needed changes objectively.

- **In general, tackle revisions from the start of the document to the end.** That is, unless a major change needs to happen in the document which could have a domino effect on other parts. In which case, tackle those first.

- **Sprint-edit your way to a finished document.** I usually take a day to make my revisions and record the following after each sprint: how many pages I edited, and how many words I subtracted or added. Unless I sprint-edit, I find that I waste too much time on other things when I could just finish my revisions and get on with my life.

- **Do another read-through.** Run spell- and grammar-check, and have another beta-read if you are bootstrapping. A proofreader can obviously give you a cleaner final copy. A small circle of advanced reviewers could also give helpful feedback at this point.

- **Savor the moment and go on to the next step: formatting your document.** Way to go! You got her done!

13

FORMAT YOUR BOOK

After publishing nearly 30 books, I now realize that formatting would go so much smoother if I hadn't left it as an after-thought.

For my first novel, *Ghost Moon Night*, I hired a formatting service, and I'm glad I did. With all the stress of my upcoming launch, I didn't want to worry about my book looking bad or worry about taking a crash course on design.

As I took on more projects, however, I taught myself how to format books to A) save money and B) be able to make changes as much as I want to when I want to.

If this is your first foray into publishing, you'd be wise to consider hiring a formatter. Prices have gone down considerably over the years, making this option more affordable. However, if you are feeling particularly brave, you can certainly bootstrap and DIY this step. You will find many tutorials online.

That said, formatting non-fiction books can be trickier than formatting fiction. For one, there are usually numbered or bulleted lists, and unless they are formatted just right for Kindle, they could look off to the average reader.

At first I formatted *Rapid Release* on Word, encountering some issues. And then I bit the bullet, bought a refurbished MacBook Air for $400, and bought the formatting software Vellum for $200. Total game-changer. It's been worth the $600 total investment for me. Vellum is user-friendly and literally takes 15 minutes to format a book on it.

Here are other steps to make formatting easier:

- **When you first start your document, set your Chapter number and title as "Heading 1" and "Heading 2" respectively.** Also designate how you want the rest of the text to look like under "Normal." This will save you gobs of time later.

- **Format the book for paperback.**
  For fiction, I usually wait "when I get around to it." Non-fiction is a different animal. Paperback can be a good source of double-sales, where someone reads it as an e-book and then purchases the physical copy. Not to mention sales period. It is beneficial to make paperback available from the get-go as I will explain towards the end of this chapter.

For reference, *Rapid Release* at 20K words was formatted with all the margins at .5, and I chose the 5" x 8" size. For another reference, I had to tweak one of my novellas, *The Heiress and the Billionaire*, at 12K words and make the text larger and double-spaced so that the paperback spine would be big enough for the title. Pull the file into Vellum later, and it will convert your file easily into an ebook. If all of this techie talk is making you sweat bullets, relax. Again, there are plenty of tutorials on formatting online, or, as already suggested earlier, outsource this part to a pro.

- **Read the ebook in your preferred**

digital format. To confirm that the formatting works for ebook, I send the file to my Kindle and read it from front to back, noting typos or last-minute changes in the Notes.

That's it. You can do this. Formatting your own books is a skill worth developing. And when you see your baby in both ebook and paperback formats, that you did all on your own, there's nothing like it!

A Note on Paperbacks

Non-fiction readers love paperbacks, especially for how-tos. Personally, I like being able to flip pages or bookmark a physical book when I am studying up on how to do something. I have also noticed my paperback sales for my non-fiction do better than fiction. So you might be leaving money on the table if you don't provide a paperback option fairly close to when you launch your ebook.

Luckily, formatting a paperback cover is also Google-able. It took me a day or two to figure out how to make mine, but if I can do it, you can too. The key to a successful paperback is to allow time to order a proof and look it over from front to back and make the necessary adjustments.

Giving your readers a paperback option not only nets you income with a potentially higher profit margin than an ebook, but paperbacks also make for great promotional tools. Since they are relatively inexpensive to print (about $2 for a 20K-word book), they could function as a business card and open doors for you.

Here's a fun little anecdote about paperbacks. After *Rapid Release* came out, a friend from my alma mater who now works for a different university invited me to teach an adult learning class. His department bought copies of my paperback which my students used as the class textbook.

I won't dwell too much on audiobooks here, as I have not personally commissioned any for my non-fiction, but with the heightened interest in podcasts in recent years, there is also greater demand for non-fiction audiobooks. Be sure to look into audio as you finalize your launch.

14

LAUNCH YOUR BOOK AS A BESTSELLER

Yes, you read that right. You can totally launch your book into an Amazon bestseller list. And not just in some obscure category, but one that might even be more competitive among books of heavy hitters. I know because it happened to me with *Rapid Release.*

Imagine that time back when there were no books on my topic yet. Everyone talked about rapid release and churned out books, but they were understandably too busy to write a book about the process. So basically, I had a book that filled a void. February proved to be a good month to launch a self-help book, still coming upon the heel of New Year's resolutions.

Here are some other things that may have helped launch *Rapid Release* into an Amazon bestselling list:

1. As an unknown in the field, I decided to

launch the book at 99 cents. That made it appealing to a voracious audience who might not otherwise have given my book a chance.

2. I formed a rapid release author group which helped established my platform among a potential audience for my book. I did it in the spirit of helping others learn alongside me, and I love seeing the cooperation and friendships in the group.

3. I hosted an Amazon giveaway of 30 ebook copies to my rapid release author group which helped my sales stats but also formed a great review crew right at the start. At 99 cents each gifted book, my small investment paid off.

4. I shared about my book, plus some especially good reviews on social media, extending its sales tail. After I shared it with other authors in some groups, my sales spiked enough to get me an Amazon top 100 ranking in the business and investment category. The next day, I raised the price to $2.99 and I fell off the charts but it was exciting while it lasted. You can read more about my launch strategy and results in Chapter 16.

Since then, I occasionally will get the little orange Amazon bestselling tag. Without any paid advertising. Why no paid advertising? Frankly, because I haven't had the time to jump into it yet. But it's encouraging to see a book do well despite not being advertised. Again, I think a lot of that has to do with the topic.

1. I made a Facebook timeline cover featuring *Rapid Release*, which kept it front and center with authors I interacted with.
2. I started a weekly author Q&A at the end of which I linked to *Rapid Release* on Amazon.

What do these results prove? If you have the right book for a hungry market at the right time, it will literally sell itself. Not only that, but I loved getting my book into the hands of authors that needed help.

To launch or not to launch at 99 cents? Keep it exclusively in Kindle Unlimited (KU) or leave it wide (available on other platforms such Apple Books or Kobo)? Read Chapter 16 to read about my launch and actual revenue stats at different price points and in KU.

~

How to get an Amazon bestselling flag
Adapted from my blog post February 7, 2019

Rapid Release had been out for two weeks, earning a #1 New Release flag out the gate simply from me sharing on social media. But I noticed that other books had a bestseller flag. I wondered what it would take to get one for my book. I had been itching to take it out of its 99 cent price point. Should I hold out and wait?

In an author group, I asked, "What does it take to get a bestselling flag on Amazon?" Someone answered, if you place #1 in any Amazon category.

As a follow-up, an author friend advised looking at the category where it ranked highest to learn the #1 book's rank. That was the number to beat, which made complete sense.

Authorship was the category I could try to place #1, but I would have to sell quite a few books before I could move the needle. RR was in the 8,000s, while the #1 book was in the low 7000s. I planned to run a Facebook ad, but I knew trying to lower the rank would be tough. I also didn't want to spend too much money on it since it was already a loss leader at 99c.

I wanted that bestseller flag mainly for visibility. I mean, it sounds cool and all, but if I could keep its rank up and pique a potential buyer's curiosity because of the flag, then that might grow sales.

I looked at rankings of other books alongside mine and discovered a category called "Alphabets." That was not as competitive a category as Authorship. But putting my writing how-to in Alphabets sounded strange. I didn't see what that had to do with my book. However, Electronic Publishing was promising.

So one evening, before I went to City Council, I emailed KDP to add my book to the Electronic Publishing category. By the time I returned home two hours later, my book had been added to that category and had earned #1 best seller status.

To some, this might seem like gaming the system, but it is a perfectly legitimate way to improve a book's ranking. Especially since I put it in categories that still made sense for my book.

My biggest takeaway: to gain visibility as a best-seller, tweak your categories by paying attention to what other books are ranking alongside your book. I plan to apply this to my future novel launches.

15

AVOID THE PITFALLS

Publishing a book on a topic of wide interest opens you up potentially to both success and criticism.

When I first published *Rapid Release,* I joined a popular author's non-fiction mastermind group and shared about my positive experience, only to be ridiculed and demeaned. I immediately left the group, feeling shaken to the core.

A few Amazon reviews were so negative (and I thought overall petty, but maybe I am just biased, ha ha) that I stopped reading them altogether without my husband first screening them. But along with those negative reviews, there were encouraging comments from authors that thanked me for sharing my rapid release experience in an honest and straightforward way.

I did try to learn from the reviews. I appreciated

those that may have been harsh but I thought were fair. For example, someone complained about formatting issues. A few weeks into publishing the book, I bought the formatting program Vellum and reformatted the ebook to give my readers a better experience.

Ironically, one of the things I didn't prepare for was the success that my little book enjoyed. Unlike my rapid release fiction stories, I had no follow-up book. No series plan. Nothing to offer readers who might already be primed for additional how-to books in a similar vein.

If I were to do things over again, I would have at least a three-book series planned, with pre—orders set up both to capture an already warm audience, and also to kick me into writing the next one.

So here I am a little over a year later since I published *Rapid Release*. I am still getting some sales and KU reads. Here's hoping that this new publication, plus any successive releases, will allow me to regain some momentum I've lost.

But it's okay, authors live and learn. And maybe, if you work hard to create your good luck, you'll get to write about it in your next book.

16

CASE STUDY: LAUNCHING RAPID RELEASE

Adapted from my blog post on April 14, 2019

Someone asked me, "I see your non-fiction book *Rapid Release* is in Kindle Unlimited (KU), and this bucks the trend for non-fiction. I'm curious what your experience has been with that, and if you'd recommend it? And most of all, what sort of 'borrow to buy' ratio do you get?"

As I have been curious myself about how my non-fiction experience has gone since publishing Rapid Release on January 19, 2019, I decided to study my stats and share my observations in a blog post.

But first, a little bit about the genesis of this book. There were four main reasons why I wrote it.

To begin with, I had data from five months of rapid releasing a clean billionaire romance series—an average of 50k words per book per month, religiously on pre-orders from August 24 (my birthday) through December 24, 2018—and I thought, why not share it? Next, whenever I would visit author forums, writers would ask about rapid release. Respondents would direct them to write-ups about it online, but none in a book. I hoped to fill that need. Third, I wanted to produce a how-to book that I wished I could have had when I started rapid releasing. Last, I'd already been blogging about my experience, so putting it all together in a book was an easy next step.

When it was all said and done, *Rapid Release* came in at 20k words or 101 e-pages. It also includes guest commentary from other authors who've successfully rapid released which I believe has given readers even more value.

Okay, so with that little background out of the way, let's look at publishing stats. Note that the only advertising I paid for was a $20 Facebook ad I ran for four days ($5 per day) in February.

Launching at 99 cents and Kindle Unlimited (KU)

. . .

I launched *Rapid Release* in the wee hours of January 19, 2019. It was a Sunday so I kept the launch on a low-down and didn't promote it actively. I began to actively promote it the following day (Monday).

Now to address the question of this book bucking the trend of non-fiction being sold "wide" on multiple platforms such as Amazon, Barnes & Noble, etc., and instead, I had decided to sell it exclusively on KU...

If you look at most writing how-to books, especially those written by indie superstars, they are sold wide and very few are on KU. Prices fluctuate anywhere from 4.99 to 9.99. If I had a more established name in non-fiction (or fiction for that matter), I would have considered upping the price to $4.99. Some, like mine, are priced at $2.99. A few that have stayed sticky (ranking high) are priced at .99, perhaps as a loss leader to funnel readers to the rest of their series.

Initially, I priced *Rapid Release* at 99 cents and not in KU. Two days later, I enrolled it in KU.

Here was my thought process on why I did the latter. I figured readers might give an unknown non-fiction author like me a chance in KU. I also thought about my behavior as a consumer. I love it when I can read a how-to book on KU, cheapskate that I am, but I don't have guilt because at least I am still giving an author page-reads.

On January 21, I enrolled the book in KU. Sales and page reads spiked that day. For 11 days, I made $117.83, selling 229 units and getting 8,366 page reads (equivalent to 82 units). Blue (top line) is KU and pink (bottom line) is sales.

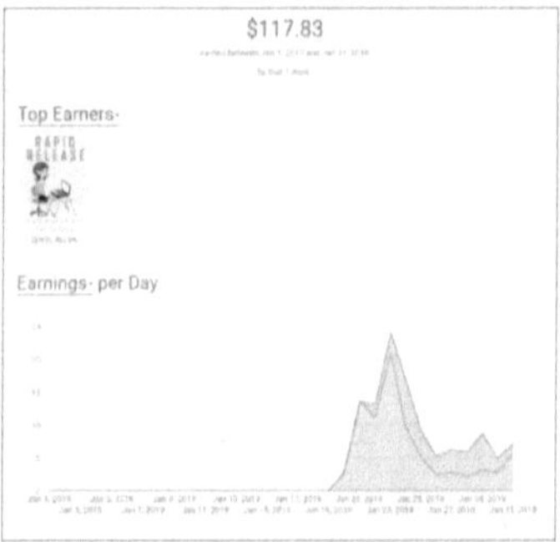

In February, I made $691.30, sold 503, and got 36,577 page reads (equivalent to 362 units). Midway through the month (more about this below the graphic) I bumped the price up to $2.99.

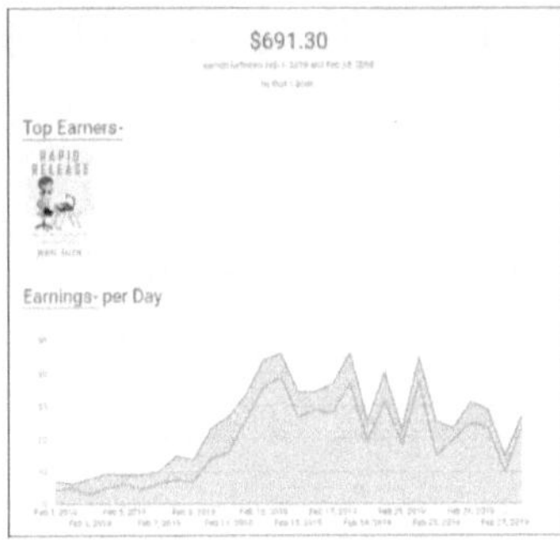

Note the spike on Feb. 13. That was when I broke into the Amazon Author rank Top 100 in Business & Investing.

What I did: I ran a $5/day Facebook ad four days that week, shared it in my newsletter and another non-fiction author's, and on social media. For a book that was an in-betweener to my fiction, I was pleasantly surprised for it to be doing so well with hardly any paid advertising.

The following day, Feb. 14, I changed the price to $2.99. I immediately lost my Amazon Author rank, but it was fun while it lasted. As you will see, the book still kept going strong despite the higher price. I decided to keep it there for the time being.

On February 21, Brian Meeks released his book *Mastering Amazon Descriptions*. *Rapid Release* appeared in its also boughts (other books his buyers have bought), which I believe gave my book a little boost.

In March, I made $616.16, sold 263 copies and had 26,437 page reads (261 units). Incidentally, I got a little spike at the end of the month. On March 28, UK-based *The Guardian* (without any prompting on my part) mentioned me and *Rapid Release* in an interesting article. The bulk of the article talked about plagiarism and its rise from the pressures of releasing fast.

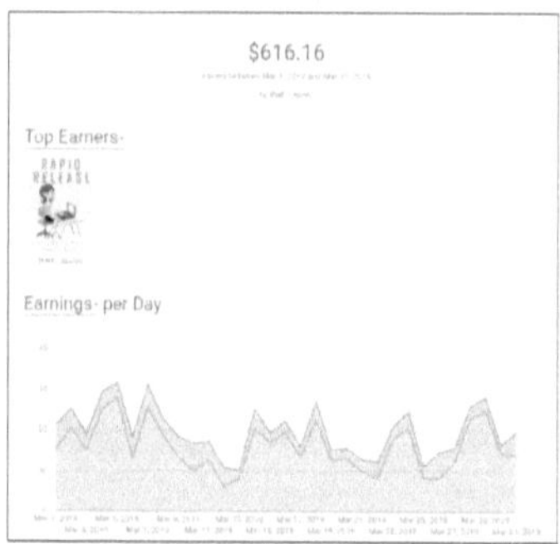

My takeaways

1.Just like with fiction, if you have more than one non-fiction book idea in you, capitalize on the interest by having others in the pipeline. *Rapid Release* made up easily half my monthly income. It would have been nice to have other titles ready.

· · ·

2.Pricing at 99 cents coupled with Facebook advertising can launch your non-fiction book into bestseller status and give you an author rank. I want to try Facebook advertising once again and see what that does. My observation as I have poked around is there is less competition in non-fiction as there is in fiction so getting that bestseller tag is easier.

3.Switching to a higher price point did not drive away readers and instead gave me more income. I loved the higher rank, but my actual royalties were smaller at 99 cents. I might try a different non-fiction title at 99 cents for longer next time to test my theory. Some readers have also commented that after they read my book in KU, they went on to buy my book at $2.99 and even recommended it for others to purchase. So I got paid both ways.

I could probably increase the price and still make sales, but I like giving a break to authors strapped for cash. $2.99 for a short non-fiction how-to seemed fair while still helping out those who may benefit from my book.

· · ·

4.Publishing non-fiction related to your fiction could help sales of the latter. I am seeing a carry-over in reads to my clean billionaire romance series because of *Rapid Release*.

5.Reviews on non-fiction could be more brutal than on fiction. Or at least I tend to take them a bit more personally. For the most part, my book has gotten 5 and 4 star reviews. And then there are a few super-harsh ones. Not surprisingly, by writing about my experience and having the chutzpah as a small fish in a big pond, I was opening myself up to criticism. However, my negative non-fiction reviews were harsher than I have seen with my fiction.

I love the good reviews while the bad ones leave me down and very insecure as a writer for a day or two. So my solution has been to stop reading reviews for now. Writing non-fiction / memoir is not for the faint-hearted.

6. That said, the positive feedback has been heart-warming and humbling. Am I glad I published *Rapid Release* despite the occasional low-blow negative

review? Definitely! I'm grateful I could help others. One of the things I never expected from publishing this book is getting messages from fellow authors who had been intimidated by self-publishing or had been ready to give up, thanking me for writing *Rapid Release* and telling me I'd given them hope.

17

BREAKING THE RULES BY ROBERT J. RYAN

Robert J. Ryan is the author of the Self-Publishing Guide series, which provides advanced publishing and marketing techniques for Indie Authors. Join his Facebook page Author Unleashed where members discuss professional-level copywriting for blurbs, newsletters, author bios, etc. and running profitable Amazon ads.

I broke all the rules...

But it still worked.

Toward the end of 2019, I launched a series of non-fiction books. I knew my target audience – other indie authors trying to come to grips with the challenges of book marketing. I knew there was a gap in the market, too.

All the books that existed in the copywriting, book blurb and Amazon ad spheres were designed to appeal to a wide audience. They were for beginners. They were entry level. Their intent was to help new self-publishers navigate the basics.

There were no advanced guides. Being a professional copywriter by background, and now a fulltime author, I knew there were a lot of people who had moved beyond the basics. They knew how to set up a Sponsored Product ad. Or that a blurb was sales copy. What they didn't have was an advanced guide that started where the other books ended.

I shunned the basics, and I delved into deep layers of expertise. This was a risk because it was a smaller niche.

But it's also a risk to place a product on the market that isn't different from existing products. You want a unique selling proposition. You want market differentiation. If you don't have that, you're at risk of sinking into the swamp.

I took this a step farther. Not only did I target a different niche from my competition, I outright challenged many of the standard practices advised by my competitors. I felt they were wrong. I had the expertise as a professional copywriter and fulltime author to say they were wrong. And to prove it.

That market differentiation worked. I have a lot of great reviews, especially on the ad book where I turned conventional wisdom on its head. People were ready for a new approach. Especially those who had learned the basics, been through the ringer and wanted more because what they had been doing wasn't working.

The key lesson here is to know your audience. Know what they've read before. Understand their problems and offer a solution that's somehow unique. You also need the inner conviction of your beliefs. If not, the reader will detect that. Sales will be lower and reviews worse.

What I did worked. The book series sold, and it sold very nicely. It's still selling over half a year later. But my targeting wasn't perfect.

My last book was on sales copy. Specifically, the neuroscience of persuasion. This book is advanced, even for professional copywriters. While there's good information in that book about backmatter, author bios, newsletters and a lot of other things that help authors convert sales, it was too advanced for the target market.

Not only that, it didn't solve a problem that most authors have. Blurbs? Authors hate writing them. Amazon ads? Authors struggle. But sales copy ... it's a bit vague. What specific problem is it solving?

That book hasn't sold as well as the others, and it's a lesson I learned. And a valuable one.

So, my golden rule is now this: Reach a specific market, in a unique way, solving an explicit problem.

I said I broke all the rules. That's probably an exaggeration, because from the above it's clear that I got some things right.

But this is food for thought. When I launched, I had no platform. None. Zero. I didn't have a blog, email list or Facebook group. I sold from scratch, relying only on the book package (title, cover, blurb, preview) and Amazon ads to sell.

It was touch and go, at first. I broke the no platform rule because, like a lot of authors, I had to. Not because having a platform is bad.

I was also hoping BookBub ads would work. They work brilliantly for fiction, but in my non-fiction genre, not so much. Or not at all. Facebook ads might have worked, but I didn't use them.

So, here's a tip. Launch from a platform if you can. Research your ad options better than I did. Be ready to go with as much firepower as you can muster.

Anyway, momentum built. Additional releases in the series fed it. The books took off and sold well.

I broke another rule. Not only did I start with no platform, I actively chose not to build a newsletter list. Instead, at the end of the books, I urge people to join the Facebook group (Author Unleashed) I'd started. So, now, I do have a platform. It's thriving, and as of today is 1,240 strong and growing by about 30 members a week.

I know everyone says you must have an email list. I certainly do for fiction. But non-fiction, I'm not so sure. A Facebook group offers so much more chance for interaction and relationship building.

It's possible that Facebook might close my account for some reason, and I'll lose my platform. But the chances of that ever happening are low. I'll take the risk. You may not want to.

I did get lucky in all this.

Recently, David Gaughran recommended me in his newsletter. That was a blast of sales, and it was the icing on the cake. (Thanks, David!).

But the idea is to make your own luck. Have a good product. Target it to a specific audience in a specific way. Solve a specific problem that resonates with the audience.

One more note. There are four books in the series, but I didn't write them rapidly. I wrote them in-between my normal fiction-writing routine. But I stored them up, and when I was ready, I released them rapidly. That was a large factor in gathering momentum and selling.

There you have it. You can break the rules and succeed. You can get lucky, too. But you always want to be working to a good plan.

. . .

Check out Robert J. Ryan's Self-Publishing Guide series and his Facebook page Author Unleashed.

18

PARTING WORDS

Overall, publishing a non-fiction how-to book has been a positive experience and has opened doors for me.

I have connected with other authors around the world as we've come together while learning about rapid releasing. Thanks to the synergy of my mastermind and reader groups, my books are also getting additional exposure overall.

As I mentioned in an earlier chapter, a university has reached out to me about teaching a class on publishing fast for profit. I also have the ability, if I want, to apply for teaching opportunities at conferences because I already have a tried and true blueprint I can share with others.

Best of all, I am happy to be able to share my experiences to hopefully inspire and help others.

Whatever stage you are at on this journey of

publishing a non-fiction book, I know you can do it too! Have faith in yourself, trust your instincts, and take the first step.

Connect with me at **www.JewelAllen.com** or on my Facebook page (Jewel Allen). Subscribe to my newsletter at **www.JewelAllen.com/subscribe** where I share free writing tips and publishing updates. Let me know how you're doing with your book project.

Thanks for reading. If you enjoyed this book, I would love for you to leave a review!

ABOUT THE AUTHOR

Jewel Allen is an award-winning journalist, author & ghostwriter who grew up in the tropics (Manila, Philippines) and now lives in the desert (Utah, USA). Visit her website at www.JewelAllen.com.